ENCYCLOPEDIA

Life in the

1950s
and 1960s

Alan Farmer

This encyclopedia is about the 1950s
and 1960s in Britain. This was a
time when many of your parents, or
grandparents, were children. In
some ways, their life then was very
different to your life today. But in
other ways it was similar.

Acknowledgements

Photos

Popperfoto, cover, page 3 bottom right, page 4 bottom, page 8 bottom, page 10 bottom, page 12 top, page 13 top, page 14 bottom, page 15 bottom, page 16 bottom, page 18 bottom, page 19 top and page 21 top. Barnaby's Picture Library, page 3 top, page 20 bottom. Advertising Archives, page 3 bottom left. Topham Picturepoint, page 4 top, page 5 bottom, page 6 bottom, page 7 bottom, page 10 top, page 14 top, page 15 bottom, page 20 top, page 22 bottom and page 23 bottom. Hulton Getty Picture Collection Ltd, page 5 top, page 13 bottom and page 23 top. Alan Farmer, page 6 top. Hulton Deutsch Collection Ltd, page 7 top, page 8 top, page 9 top and bottom, page 11 top, page 17 top, page 18 top and page 19 bottom. Hulton Deutsch Collection/Corbis, page 9 top and bottom, page 19 bottom. Fox Photos Ltd, page 11 bottom. FPG International/C. J. Zimmerman, page 12 bottom. FPG International/C. Willinger, page 15 top. Press Association/ Topham Picturepoint, page 16 top. Mary Evans Picture Library/Henry Grant, page 17 bottom. Keystone Press Agency Ltd, page 21 bottom. Corbis-Bettamann/UPI, page 22 top.

Heinemann Educational Publishers
Halley Court, Jordan Hill, Oxford OX2 8EJ
a division of Reed Educational & Professional Publishing Ltd

OXFORD FLORENCE PRAGUE MADRID ATHENS
MELBOURNE AUCKLAND KUALA LUMPUR SINGAPORE TOKYO
IBADAN NAIROBI KAMPALA JOHANNESBURG GABORONE
PORTSMOUTH NH (USA) CHICAGO MEXICO CITY SAO PAULO

© Reed Educational & Professional Publishing Ltd 1997

First published 1997

02 01 00 99 98

10 9 8 7 6 5 4 3 2

British Library Cataloguing in Publication Data
A catalogue record for this book is available from the British Library.

ISBN 0 435 09563 3   *Encyclopedia of Life in the 1950s and 1960s*
                        individual copy pack: 6 copies of 1 title
ISBN 0 435 09415 7   Stage E pack: 1 each of 7 titles

Colour reproduction by Reacta Graphics.

Printed and bound in Great Britain by Scotprint.

Cars and scooters

In the 1950s, there were not many cars on the roads. A car was too expensive for most people to buy. They used trams or bicycles instead.

By the 1960s, more people owned cars. The most common car was the Mini. It was small and cheap to run. Some people liked to travel about on scooters.

Celebrations

In 1953, Princess Elizabeth was crowned Queen Elizabeth II. Many people watched her coronation on television. Tea parties were held in the streets to celebrate. School children were given a coronation mug, with the Queen's picture on.

In 1966-67, Francis Chichester was the first person to sail around the world alone. His yacht was called *Gipsy Moth IV*. In celebration, he was knighted by Queen Elizabeth II.

Cinema and radio

At the start of the 1950s, not many people had a television. Many people listened to the radio. The cinema was very popular. People waited in long queues to see the latest film.

By the 1960s, most houses had a television. Fewer people visited the cinema. Radios were smaller, so they could be carried easily. They were called portable transistors.

Clothes

1950s

Men often wore dark suits with shirts and ties. Boys wore short trousers. Women and girls wore dresses and skirts. Lots of people wore hats.

1960s

In the 1960s, many people wore bright and colourful clothes. Some men grew their hair long. Young women wore short skirts called mini-skirts. This time was called the 'swinging sixties'.

Electrical machines

In the 1950s, not many people had electrical machines. Washing was usually done by hand. It was hard work and often took the whole day to do.

By the 1960s, homes had lots of electrical machines. They used washing machines, cookers and fridges. They also used vacuum cleaners, televisions and electrical fires.

Environment

1950s Most houses and factories used coal fires. There was a lot of smoke in the air. Big towns sometimes had smogs. Smogs are a mixture of smoke and fog. Smogs made it difficult to breathe.

1960s In the 1960s, people in towns had to use smokeless coal. This stopped the smogs. But there were now more cars on the roads. The cars filled the air with exhaust fumes.

Families

In the early 1950s, many homes were shared by grandparents, parents and children. Most women stayed at home to look after the family.

By the 1960s, most married couples lived on their own with their children. Many women went back to work after their children had started school.

Football

1950s

Football matches were very popular. Large crowds watched matches. Most people had to stand up to watch the game.

1960s

In 1966, England won the World Cup. The final score was England: 4, West Germany: 2. In 1967, Glasgow Celtic were the first British team to win the European Cup.

Health

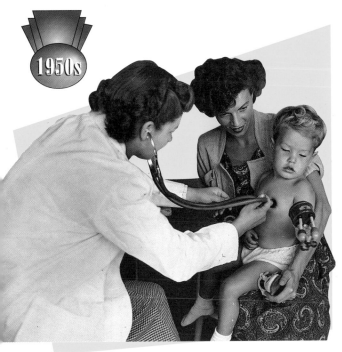

People were more healthy than they had been in the 1940s. The National Health Service started in 1948. People did not have to pay to see the doctor or dentist.

In the 1960s, doctors learnt how to replace a heart or kidney. People were healthier and lived longer than ever before. Many people smoked cigarettes and pipes. They did not know that smoking was bad for their health.

Holidays

 1950s Most holidays were spent at the seaside in Britain. People wore their smart suits and dresses on the beach.

 1960s

Holiday camps and caravanning became very popular. By the middle of the 1960s, many people flew to other countries, like Spain, for their holidays.

Houses

1950s Many homes had been destroyed in the Second World War. There were not enough houses for people to live in. Some families lived in temporary houses, called prefabs. Large housing estates were built.

1960s In the 1960s, tall tower blocks were built in many cities for families to live in. They had no gardens, so children often had nowhere to play.

Machines

1950s

Computers were huge. They were so big that they took up whole rooms. No one had a computer at home because they were too large.

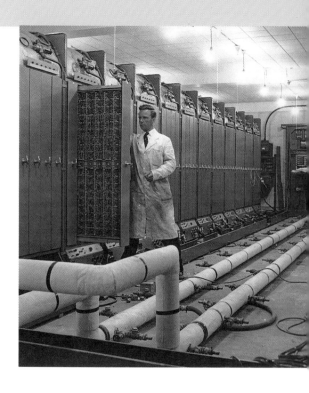

1960s

In the 1960s, tape recorders were used in offices and homes. They were large and heavy. They were the size of a small suitcase.

Music

1950s

Young people listened to their favourite music on the radio. They bought records and played them at home on record players. They liked rock and roll music. American singers, like Elvis Presley and Buddy Holly, were very popular.

1960s

The most popular British group in the 1960s was the Beatles. Their fans screamed with excitement when they played their music. They were famous all over the world.

15

Playing games

There were only a few cars on the roads in the 1950s. Children often played games in the side streets. Boys played football and cricket. Girls enjoyed skipping and hopscotch.

By the 1960s, there were lots of cars on the roads. Children could no longer play in the street. New parks and playgrounds were built. They had swings, slides and roundabouts.

School

1950s Children had to work very hard at school. There was an exam they had to take when they were 11 years old. It was called the 11+. It decided which school they would go to next.

1960s In the 1960s, many new schools were built. School classrooms were lighter and brighter. Fewer children took the 11+ exam.

Shopping

1950s People usually went shopping every day for fresh food. The shops were small and the shop-keeper would serve customers over

the counter. The shops were often in the same street where people lived.

1960s Large supermarkets opened in many towns. They sold lots of different things.

Customers served themselves from the shelves. Many of the small shops were forced to close because they were more expensive than the supermarkets.

Television

Televisions showed black and white pictures during the 1950s.

In the 1960s, many more families had televisions. In 1967, colour television started. The first colour televisions cost a lot of money.

Toys and comics

In the 1950s, children had bikes and scooters. They played with train sets, toy soldiers, dolls and prams. Most children read comics like 'The Dandy' and 'The Beano'.

In the 1960s, more toys were made from plastic. There were many more toys and comics to choose from.

Transport

1950s People in towns used buses and trams to travel around. Longer journeys were made by steam trains.

1960s Steam trains were replaced by diesel trains. Luxury coaches and buses were used for long-distance travel. Many railway lines were closed because they were not being used.

Travelling abroad

1950s Most people who wanted to visit another country in the 1950s had to travel by sea. This meant long journeys on a ship. It would take five or six weeks to get to countries like Australia.

1960s In the 1960s, bigger and faster aeroplanes were built, like Concorde and the Jumbo jet. This made travelling to other countries easier and quicker.

Work

1950s It was easy for most people to find work. Most young people went straight from school into a job. Some women learnt typing and worked in offices. Many women stopped working when they got married.

1960s In the 1960s, many people worked in modern factories. Machines did some of the work. More women stayed at work when they were married.

Index